Betty Shine was born in Kennington in 1929. Her grandmother was a spiritualist. Before she became a practising healer, she was a professional singer, and she has at times taught vitamin and mineral therapy, hand analysis and yoga. She lives and practises in the south of England. Her first three books, Mind to Mind, Mind Magic *and* Mind Waves *are all available in Corgi.*

Also by Betty Shine

MIND TO MIND
MIND MAGIC
MIND WAVES

and published by Corgi Books

BETTY SHINE'S MIND WORKBOOK

EXERCISES LINKING MIND, BODY AND SPIRIT

CORGI BOOKS

BETTY SHINE'S MIND WORKBOOK
A CORGI BOOK : 0 552 14214 X

First publication in Great Britain

PRINTING HISTORY
Corgi edition published 1994

5 7 9 10 8 6

Some of the exercises which appear in this book have been
published in *Mind to Mind*, *Mind Magic* or *Mind Waves*.

Set in 11/14pt Linotype New Baskerville by
Phoenix Typesetting, Ilkley, West Yorkshire.

Corgi Books are published by Transworld Publishers,
61–63 Uxbridge Road, London W5 5SA,
a division of The Random House Group Ltd,
in Australia by Random House Australia (Pty) Ltd,
20 Alfred Street, Milsons Point, Sydney, NSW 2061, Australia,
in New Zealand by Random House New Zealand Ltd,
18 Poland Road, Glenfield, Auckland 10, New Zealand
and in South Africa by Random House (Pty) Ltd,
Endulini, 5a Jubilee Road, Parktown 2193, South Africa.

Printed and bound in Great Britain by
Clays Ltd, St Ives plc.

To all the healing groups worldwide

CONTENTS

MANTRAS

FOREWORD

Why a workbook? Over the past five years I have received thousands of letters from around the world thanking me for writing my three books *Mind to Mind, Mind Magic* and *Mind Waves*. Healing, Meditation, Yoga Groups, and many more have been inspired by the exercises that I included in those books.

My readers have also enjoyed the quotations and poems and have repeatedly requested more. I have, too, been asked for ideas for tackling the positive and negative sides of our nature. Something simple.

But most of all, readers have asked how I could simplify their lives. As one lady wrote, 'Your exercises are wonderful and they really work but I haven't the time to flick through all three books all the time.' When a close friend made the same observation she also gave me an idea, 'Why not write a workbook?' A brilliant idea I thought, so here it is.

Not only have I extracted the exercises from my three books, I have also added new ones which I am sure will be as popular as the others. There is a blank feedback page-spread after every exercise so that you can keep a record of your progress. Eventually, you may find that certain exercises are more beneficial to you than others.

Quotations and poems have been added, as well as charts for positive and negative observations and many other ideas.

An exercise called 'The Magician's Castle' which I have always used with friends for self-analysis and clairvoyance is also included. Make of it what you will: it changes every time it is used and the magic never ceases to amaze me. I know you will have as much fun with your friends as I have had with this one.

The real power of this book will eventually be of your own making. Every observation you make will be of great value later on. Your emotions will be recorded, your progress will be recorded and you will learn how to turn your negativity around and make it work for you. This book will represent the real you, and I know you will be surprised at what you will find out about yourself. When writing in this book always remember, 'To thine own self be true'.

The main exercises have no order. The idea behind that decision is that so many of my readers have been amazed when they have opened one of my books at random and realized that the page that appeared to them was exactly what they needed for that day. So why not allow your intuition to work for you and do the same? Your higher mind is well aware of your needs!

You will realize also, as you turn the pages of this book, that there is a feeling of freedom, of space. You will find quotations containing perhaps only two lines centred on a blank page. I have structured it this way so that it will be easy to retain the thought. When you have done so the page will not be blank, it will reflect your own thoughts. There is always so much more than the written word if we care to seek it out.

The linking of Mind, Body and Spirit is the main aim. I hope you enjoy the workbook as much as I have enjoyed writing it.

I am indebted to my daughter, Janet Shine, for additional exercises and mantras that were used in her yoga classes with such excellent results.

Make this your own private manual by choosing a favourite photograph of yourself and pasting it on this blank page

Lost, yesterday, somewhere between
Sunrise and Sunset, two golden hours,
each set with sixty diamond minutes.
No reward is offered, for they are
gone for ever.

HORACE MANN 1796–1859
'Lost, Two Golden Hours'

LIFE

All life is a challenge. Once you have acquired your new optimistic outlook nothing can stop you. Every day is a challenge. The mind, once free, will ebb and flow joining the Universal Mind. Your intuition will be second to none. Intuitively, you will be doing and saying the right things. You will become a part of all dimensions. Awareness will become the driving force behind every activity, be it work or play. Follow your intuition, do not argue with it. You will be surprised at how right you can be.

Behold, I do not give lectures
or a little charity,
When I give I give myself.

WALT WHITMAN 1819–92

THE ENERGY COUNTERPART
EXPLAINED

All life is energy, and fitting neatly into the physical system is the ENERGY COUNTERPART, which mirrors it on the non-physical plane. The aura – a word much used but little understood – is an extension of the energy counterpart. It protrudes about an inch and a half all round the physical body when the latter is healthy and, along with the energy counterpart, virtually disappears and becomes invisible when it is not. A unique gift that has been bestowed upon me is the ability to 'see' this energy. The most important components of the energy counterpart are the vortices, or chakras, to give them their Hindu name, and meridian lines.

The vortices appear opposite the ductless glands in the endocrine system. Their function is to draw in life force and stimulate the glands' hormonal output. When the body is healthy these vortices spin at great speed. When it is sick they begin to slow down, drawing in life force at a diminishing rate and setting up a vicious circle. For if, as already explained, our mind energy begins to funnel inwards instead of expanding outwards, a congestion of energy gradually forms in the body, the major organs are prevented from pulsating, cells and tissues suffer and tremendous negative pressure builds up, affecting in its turn the energy counterpart and aura which, as explained, retracts into the body and becomes invisible. The healer's first task in this situation is to get the vortices spinning again. This can be done by energizing the system through healing until they are once more turning with the sparkle and speed of Catherine wheels.

As well as the vortices, the energy counterpart displays a whole network of what are known as meridian lines. These are energy lines that channel life force through the physical body. I have no idea how many meridian lines there are, but there are quite a few, some of which I have seen. To clear them I draw the energy back through the feet rather as a pipe smoker uses his pipe cleaner. This also reactivates the vortices. Acupuncture, in the hands of a skilled practitioner, has the same effect. As the needles are inserted into the physical body, they release negative congestion from the energy counterpart.

Many books offer line drawings claiming to illustrate the position of the vortices. This book will not offer you charts or sketches of anything, for the reason that I want you to exercise your imagination and, by so doing, expand your mind energy. But I recognize that many people find such visualization difficult, particularly at the start. If you are one of them, try the following exercise.

Sit down, close your eyes, and imagine that you are transparent. You can see, or imagine, an outline of your physical body. Moving down it slowly from the top front of your head, observe the first vortex spinning like a Catherine wheel. Now move to just about the middle of the forehead. Here is another vortex, slightly elongated in shape this time, but also spinning away at its centre. Now to the throat. Have another look at these three vortices. If by now your imagination is flagging, just accept that they are all there, spinning away.

Now we come to the heart vortex, at the centre of the breastbone, then to the vortex situated just over the pancreas, then to another just below it, at the level of the navel.

Now turn your energy being around, so that it has its back to you. Here is the seventh and last main vortex, situated at the base of the spine. This is the *kundalini*, the 'earth vortex', drawing its strength from the earth's energies.

So here you have, in your mind's eye, a picture of your energy counterpart, your transparent frame with its seven spinning vortices.

Now turn your energy being around to face you again and look down at its feet. Lift your gaze slowly up the body's left side, right up to the shoulder, and you will see channels of energy, maybe two or three. These are your meridian lines. Starting with the right foot and rising to the right shoulder, you will see the same thing. Perhaps it will be easier for you to visualize these channels as tubes. Now let your energy being raise its arms. From beneath the armpits there are tubes going down both arms. There are also many channels tracing a course across the chest and back and up through the neck into the head.

Vortices spinning and drawing in life force, channels or meridians distributing this life force, the whole energy being vibrating and pulsating – that is what your energy counterpart should look like and therefore how you should visualize it while controlling it.

Now, imagine you are entering this wonderful, vibrating energy being. Simply walk into it and, if it adds to your sense of security, zip yourself up at the back. Suddenly this energy will take on the shapes of all your major organs, curling around them, mimicking them, and regenerating every cell in your body. Now you are feeling on top of the world because you are fit and healthy and bubbling over with the energy.

Do not underestimate the energy counterpart or dismiss it as mere fantasy. It is not. It is as real as our physical bodies which, without it, could not exist. When our vortices are spinning we are healthy and full of life, when they are slow disease sets in and when they stop we die.

Most people jog along with slow vortices all their lives. They show little interest in how their physical bodies work, let alone their energy counterparts. But such neglect exacts a penalty and this falls due when they are ill. Then they feel out of control. Along comes the doctor with his usual well-meaning prescriptions. But the drugs he prescribes will only slow the vortices down even more, while their chemical reaction will alter the messages from the brain, thereby leading to more problems.

How much safer to play down the physical side and concentrate from the first on manipulating the energy counterpart, starting even when you are well – it is so much easier to control and the physical body will benefit as a matter of course.

All you have to remember is that there are seven vortices, perhaps more. Don't worry about where they are. Just be convinced that they exist and are spinning like Catherine wheels while drawing in life force. The same with the meridian lines. Don't worry about them. Just assure yourself that they are there and are conducting the life force around the body.

AND DO NOT EVER FORGET THAT THE MIND IS THE CONTROL TOWER.

New opinions are always suspected, and usually opposed, without any other reason but because they are not already common.

JOHN LOCKE 1632–1704
An Essay concerning Human Understanding (1690)

ABSENT HEALING EXERCISE

---

1. Find a quiet place where you will not be disturbed. Sit in a comfortable chair, close your eyes and relax. Breathe deeply three times.

2. Think of someone who is unwell. If you do not know their address, don't worry. Simply think of their name and you will automatically be there – that is if you have carried out the previous exercises correctly.

3. You are now in their home. Picture them sitting in a comfortable chair. Now place your hands on their shoulders and ask for help in their recovery. In this healing mode you may be given some information about the illness and why they are suffering from it.

4. When you feel the healing has been successful simply think yourself back home again.

5. Wait a day or two before you make any enquiries about the health of your patient.

6. Keep whatever information you may have received to yourself. All spiritual work is confidential. Keep records to guide you; this way you can judge whether or not you are making any progress.

FEEDBACK

Date ....

'Tis a lesson you should heed,
Try, try again.
If at first you don't succeed,
Try, try again.

W.E. HICKSON 1803–70
'Try and Try Again'

RELIEVING STRESS

---

1. Choose a nice, quiet room, preferably carpeted. Now lie down on the floor and close your eyes.

2. Breathe deeply three times. Try to breathe through your nose so that the air makes a slight hissing sound as you breathe in. Hold the third breath for as long as possible, then let it out in small puffs. As you do this, you will feel energy circulating throughout your body and you will begin to feel warm. You may also feel a bit light-headed, if so, do not hold your breath for so long next time. Repeat three times.

3. Now visualize energy building up underneath your body, little by little, until it is a solid mass. When you are successful with this part of the exercise, move on.

4. You will feel at this point as though you are going to levitate, and that you are in a dream-state. Forget everything and enjoy every minute. Stay with it.

FEEDBACK

———————————

Date ....

I have striven not to laugh at
human actions, not to weep at them,
nor to hate them, but to understand
them.

BARUCH SPINOZA 1632–77
Tractatus Politicus

DISCIPLINING YOUR THOUGHTS

Disciplining and channelling your thoughts can also be of immense benefit in other areas of your life. This exercise has been devised to help you in this way.

1. Choose a quiet place, sit down and relax. Breathe deeply three times. Close your eyes.

2. Think of a nursery rhyme, and visualize each word as though it was alive. Now repeat the verse in your mind and, as you do so, follow the words as they walk down a corridor. Think of them as children. If you see one of them disappearing into a door off the corridor, guide it back to the mainstream. *Remember you are always in control.*

3. When they have reached the end of the corridor – it does not matter how long it takes – bring them back again. Because the words have a mind of their own, the journey back could be very frustrating, so keep your eyes on every word-child and do not allow your mind to stray.

FEEDBACK

_____

Date ....

Lightning flashed
across the sky, and
the clouds, for one
split second, became an accumulation of
many coloured pillows.

The earth, parched and brown,
glowed like a bed of coals
as though brought to life by
giant bellows.

Not a sound could be heard,
no animal,
no bird,
no sign of any life at all,
as the flashes danced around.

A force far greater than mortals could produce,
was wandering about the heavens,
occasionally to touch the ground.

In moments such as these,
there is no doubt,
that we on earth are indeed
very small.

These signs, perhaps,
are to remind us,
that it is
only by the Grace of God,
we exist at all.

B.S.

UP IN THE CLOUDS

Sit down quietly and close your eyes. Breathe deeply three times. Now feel yourself floating peacefully out of the window. You really can imagine this in more than a fanciful sense because once more it is the mind that is doing the work in all this and the mind is energy and can pass through anything. Now you are outside and can feel yourself lift off and leave the ground, slowly at first, then gradually picking up speed. I'm sure there's a bit of Mary Poppins in all of us!

Above you are clouds. Soon you will reach them and as you do so jump on the one which you like the best and which you think will be the most comfortable. Make yourself at home on it. You can lie on your back looking up at the sky above, or lean over and look down at the earth. You will feel free and relaxed but most of all you will be at peace.

Feel the buoyancy of the cloud and its texture. Perhaps it feels like cotton wool or perhaps it is more like a beautiful piece of silk. Whatever it feels like, enjoy it. You are drifting along. If you are looking up, what do you see? Perhaps more clouds or perhaps a blue sky or perhaps it is night and you are able to study the stars. Concentrate so that you can remember every detail.

If you are lying down, what can you see as you look over the edge? Fields, towns, villages, highways, forests, rivers, lakes, mountains, churches, beacons. Whatever the sights below you, remember them.

Stay aloft on your cloud for as long as you wish. When you feel it is time to return, just think yourself down. Your cloud, when it reaches the earth, will evaporate into mist and disappear.

Now, as before, let us go through your experience.

1. Did you find lift-off difficult? If you did, you have obviously become frightened of change. But don't worry. When practising this exercise for the first few times, just skip this lift-off part and visualize yourself on the cloud. But don't skip it too often!

2. If you found lift-off easy but failed to pick up speed, this means you are cautious but still willing to have a go, so again, don't worry.

3. If, however, you went zooming away rather too fast, then you are so eager for change and excitement that you could land yourself in trouble. The best take-off starts slowly but gradually builds up speed. As you continue to practise the exercise, always strive for this middle path and little by little it will balance your personality.

4. What did your cloud look like? Was it small, big, elongated, wide or middling? If it was small, you expect very little from life and perhaps are afraid to ask for anything more. If it was big, you embrace life with open arms and expect as much love from other people as you give out. If it is elongated, you want more than your fair share and if it is fat the same thing goes. If it is middling, you are a moderate personality and perhaps also a bit staid. Why not break out now and then?

5. Did you lie on your back looking up? If you did, were there clouds above you, a blue sky, or was it night? If it was night were there stars? If there were clouds, your life is a bit hazy and this applies especially to your ideas about the future. Try to melt them away and gain more clarity of vision. A blue sky, however, is a happier indication. It suggests you have a clear idea of what you want from your life and would like to go out and get it. Why not! If it was night there is a darker side involved. You have a secretive nature and want to keep things to yourself – that is, if the night was starless. But if there were stars you have an affinity with the universe.

6. Were you lying down? What did you see below? If you saw open fields with few trees in them and few houses around, then your life at the moment is barren. At your next attempt, try to visualize more detail. If you saw forests, then your life is over-complicated. Try to thin out the trees. Or did you see lakes and mountains or a landscape with a beautiful river flowing through? Water is always an excellent thing to see, for it is spiritual and fluid like our energy bodies and our minds. Mountains also have a mystical significance, forever reaching up from the earth.

7. Did you want to go higher? If so, you are eager to investigate and break down barriers.

These exercises will probably reveal you as a mixture of opposing attitudes. Most people are. But all of them will help you to analyse yourself and to solve your problems as you practise them. You will be surprised how easy they make it to work things out.

FEEDBACK

Date ....

Music, the greatest good that mortals know,
And all of heaven we have below.

JOSEPH ADDISON 1672–1719
'A Song for St Cecilia's Day'

MUSIC: TOUCHING THE SOUL

---

1. Tune into the music of your choice. Sit on the floor with your arms around your knees. Close your eyes.

2. As you listen, rock back and forth very gently, in time with the rhythm.

3. Become aware of the vibrations within your body and allow the tensions to ease away.

4. When you feel that you are a part of the performance change position. Sit crosslegged, with the palms of your hands on your knees, eyes closed.

5. At this point you should feel light and heady. Allow yourself the freedom of being in a timeless situation. Stay in this position until the performance is finished, and give yourself a further three minutes to return to normal

   Because you have something specific to think about during the performance, your mind will not wander, and this enables you to channel your thoughts.

FEEDBACK

Date ....

PSYCHOMETRY: SECRETS OF INANIMATE OBJECTS

Psychometry can provide you with a mass of information that would probably never otherwise be divulged. It has enabled me to help people by linking into vibrations they never realized were there.

EXTRACTING SECRETS

1. Ask a friend to give you something belonging to someone unknown to you. This is important because information and pictures can be clouded by the subconscious. The owner's permission must be given before the article is used for this purpose.

2. Sit down in a comfortable chair in a quiet room. Cup the object in your hands, and close your eyes. Now relax, as though you are going to day-dream. Allow your mind to drift away from the object. *Do not even think about it.*

3. You will begin to feel sensations within your body. When this happens, link them up with *your* normal sensations. For

instance, your stomach might start to rumble when you are frightened or when you have too much acidity. Perhaps you get pains in your stomach when you are emotionally upset. If you have these symptoms whilst holding the object and you did not have them immediately before you did so, then you are picking up the owner's problems. Always relate the feelings to your own, because you are interpreting them through your own energy counterpart. Sometimes you will find that your head aches. If you do not normally suffer with headaches, then again, the owner probably does.

It might be that you simply tune into that person's personality. Consequently, you will receive the good with the bad. Whatever you do, do not judge. That is not the purpose of the exercise.

When you feel that you have absorbed as much information as possible in a time limit of ten minutes, open your eyes and relax. Whatever you do, do not continue beyond that time as it will tire you.

4. If you have a photograph, follow the same procedure, studying it occasionally. Remember the most prominent features – these are usually the eyes, and the eyes are the mirror of the soul.

When you think you have a clear picture, close your eyes again and just think about it. It can be quite amazing when the information starts to flow. Sometimes it is like ticker-tape, moving so fast that it is difficult to remember it all.

Sometimes you will receive symbolism. For instance, if you have an impression of a fast flowing river, then it is probable that the owner's life is getting out of control. It could be that you will receive pictures or impressions of a cross. Be careful with this one – it may not necessarily mean that the person is religious. It

47

might be that they may feel like a martyr.

A very common impression is of a bowl. Again this can be a tricky one. It could mean that the person will receive a gift – or that their life is like an empty bowl. It could even mean that the person is asking for help.

I have always found symbols confusing. It is much better to wait until you have very positive information and pictures. You will be on safer ground.

Whatever you do, do not make it up. You could find yourself in trouble and then your reputation will be shattered.

Enjoy your new hobby, knowing that it is increasing your sensitivity and awareness so that you will feel closer to others. The world would be in a worse state than it is at the moment without the sensitives who give love, sympathy and hope. Become one of these people. The world needs you.

FEEDBACK

Date ....

If we could rid ourselves
of 'I' we would understand
the reason why we are here
at all. It is not to ask
all the time for obedience
and love, to make others
thought forms of our imagination
but to accept they must be free
to develop their own personality,
to perhaps, just 'be'.

If we could rid ourselves of
'I' we would be releasing
ourselves, living our own lives
without fear and expectancy
of reward. Individuality and
freedom can be attained if we
could rid ourselves of 'I' and
in the giving find the ultimate
reason for living.

B.S.

WRITE IT DOWN

One way of getting rid of depression and other negative feelings is to get paper and pen and write everything down. Unhappiness, hatred, envy, despair, jealousy, resentment, vindictiveness – let all the problems that have been building up tumble out of your mind onto the paper!

Don't be afraid to own to these feelings. You are not alone; all these and more are natural feelings that tend to surface during our lives when circumstances trigger them off.

Keep writing your feelings down until you are sick of writing. Whatever you do, *don't* read through what you have written. Let it go. We are rather like computers, and reading the information would store it again. Tear the paper up into small pieces and put them in a container such as a biscuit-tin. Then set light to the paper, preferably in the fireplace or garden (if you haven't either, use the sink where you can turn the tap on if necessary!). Reduce the whole thing to ashes, and start your life afresh.

This is also an excellent way of getting rid of all the things that you'd like to say to other people, but don't dare say or don't want to hurt them with. Say them on paper, and finish with it.

You don't need all that rubbish; allowing it to build up inside you will only lead to illnesses of mind and body. Cleanse yourself of unnecessary burdens. We acquire so many that this clean-out is an absolute must, at least once a month! It will help you to be in control of your life.

Above all, enjoy it. It can be great fun!

FEEDBACK

Date ....

Possessions are material
things that give but a
moment's pleasure – and if
by material things our
success is measured then
we are a poor return for
the life we have been given,
for 'tis a very precious
gift to be used for universal
matters. In the end we must
atone and will be judged for
ourselves alone, and not by
what or whom we own.

B.S.

SMOOTHING YOUR AURA

Ever since I saw my own lopsided mind energy in the mirror, I have regularly treated myself by smoothing out my aura. Anybody can do it. Using both hands, simply stroke downwards over your head and the area around it, and then stroke down over your shoulders. You can use a soft scarf held in both hands to do your back. Then use your hands to smooth down each arm in turn, going right over the ends of your fingers, and then stroke down your body, legs and feet. This also removes toxins lying just under the surface of the skin.

FEEDBACK

Date ....

For she was beautiful – her beauty made
The bright world dim, and everything beside
Seemed like the fleeting image of a shade.

PERCY BYSSHE SHELLEY 1792–1822
'The Witch of Atlas'

MIRROR IMAGE

Sit down in a chair in a quiet room and close your eyes. A spirit helper is going to put his hands on your head and as he does so you will sense a tingling all over your body. You will then begin to feel completely relaxed. Your eyes will be closed and you will feel a heaviness in your feet slowly creeping up you until your body is 'paralysed' and you are unable to move.

You are now in a state of complete relaxation, and whatever you have wrong with you will begin to disappear. If you haven't anything wrong with you, you will still feel energy surging through your body as it is rejuvenated. If you are elderly, you will begin to feel as though you have shed many years. You will feel the circulation renewed, the blood flowing through your whole body, cleansing it, removing toxins. Your skin will feel clearer, your eyes brighter, your wrinkles will be removed. Any excess skin around the neck will tighten up, and your whole body will be tingling with the incredible feeling of health and youth.

Whatever age you are, you are now giving yourself your first Beauty Treatment of the Mind – the most wonderful beauty treatment of your life. You on your own. You are your own surgeon. Whatever you want to happen to your body will happen. You no longer feel lost and powerless to do things for yourself.

Now someone has brought you a full-length mirror. Look into

it. You will see for yourself what an incredible change has taken place. You will enjoy looking at yourself, knowing that with regular treatment the new you will emerge. Eventually you will not have to look into your imaginary mirror all the time, only when you feel the need to do so.

Take at least ten minutes to carry out this exercise. It will change your life and your looks. Believe me, it really works, for whilst you have been imagining all these changes you have been giving instructions to your body and training it to carry out the instructions of your mind. By so doing you have reversed the age process and the message will be picked up loud and clear by your body's cells. All cells have a 'mind of their own', responsive to your own mind, and will appreciate a full set of instructions.

FEEDBACK

Date ....

Tell me what you eat and I will tell you what you are.

ANTHELME BRILLAT-SAVARIN 1755–1826

STAY THE PANGS!

I had an interesting conversation with a friend of mine the other day. He was telling me about his great-uncle who was a painter, and who used to suffer from tremendous pangs of hunger from time to time. When this happened he used to paint a plate of food and then slowly rub it out. When he had finished he felt as though he had actually eaten the food. I was extremely interested in this story as it sums up what I am trying to teach. What my friend's uncle had done was to make energy food – and like everything else you make with energy, this became a reality.

If you are feeling hungry when you happen to be reading this book, try the method for yourself. Sit down, close your eyes, and imagine you are eating the most delicious foods you can think of. Taste the different flavours, savour them, see yourself enjoying them and feel your stomach filling up. If you can't visualize them just know that you are eating them. Believe me, it works. This exercise is also an ideal one for slimmers. You can have all the chocolate bars you want and never put on weight!

FEEDBACK

Date ....

If all the good people were clever,
And all clever people were good,
The world would be nicer than ever
We thought that it possibly could.
But somehow, 'tis seldom or never
The two hit it off as they should;
The good are so harsh to the clever,
The clever so rude to the good!

ELIZABETH WORDSWORTH 1840–1932
'Good and Clever'

INSTANT RECALL

This exercise is to enable you to file away information so that you can recall it at any time.

Once again I would like you to sit quietly and breathe deeply three times. Once you have done this I want you to see or know that there is a row of filing cabinets in your room. On top of the filing cabinets you will find labels and a pen. I want you to write these labels as follows: 1. Universal Mind, 2. Environment, 3. Healthy Food, 4. Vitamins and Minerals, 5. Ability to Heal, 6. Miscellaneous. These are only a few suggestions; you can write any number of labels with the titles of your choice.

Now try to remember something you have read in this book that you have found interesting and would like to remember. Make out another label to fit it (unless of course, it suits one of the above). Choose your file, open the drawer, take out a folder and file the information away. When you have replaced the folder in the file, look at the label on the front again, and remember which file it is in. Then push the drawer closed. Now you will have instant recall when you want to remember that particular piece of information. The method is simply to think of your file. Think of the label on the outside, open the file, take out the appropriate folder, and look inside. As you become more proficient all you will have to do is think of the Universal Mind and everything will be revealed!

Carry on in this way, filing away all sorts of information. It can be very interesting, especially when your mind begins to feed you with information you thought you had forgotten. This will happen more and more in response to the initial stimulus, as the process gains momentum. You will probably become an addict!

FEEDBACK

Date ....

My soul is an enchanted boat,
Which, like a sleeping swan, doth float
Upon the silver waves of thy sweet singing.

PERCY BYSSHE SHELLEY 1792–1822
Prometheus Unbound

DRIFTING

This exercise is excellent for self-analysis.

1. Breathe deeply three times.

2. Visualize a buttercup meadow, a sea of golden flowers blowing in the breeze. Feel the breeze caressing your face. Now walk through the meadow marvelling at the beauty of Nature.

3. In the distance you will see a river. At your own pace make your way to the river bank.

4. When you arrive at the bank, look down and you will see a rowing boat bobbing up and down on its mooring. Make your way down the bank and step into the boat. Inside the boat you will find a pair of oars. When you are ready untie the boat and start rowing.

5. After a while lie down in the boat and let it drift downstream. Feel the warmth of the sun on your face and listen to the skylarks. The water lapping at the side of the boat will give it a gentle rocking motion as you drift along.

6. Eventually the rowing boat will drift into the bank and stop.

7. Sit up and breathe deeply. Look around and take in the scene before you. Remember everything.

8. Now stand up and step out. If the bank is steep then you will have to climb a little. If the landing is flat, all the better.

9. You will find yourself standing in a field. The nature of this field will be of your own making.

10. You will see someone walking towards you; it may be a spiritual guide, a friend or a member of your family. They will have a message for you.

11. Alone or with your companion you will make your way towards the only tree in the field. Sit by the tree or if it's large enough, underneath, and absorb the healing aura. Stay as long as you wish.

SUMMING UP

Many people find it difficult to get into the boat. This shows that you feel your problems are insurmountable.

If you found your journey difficult and the water rough, this represents your lifestyle.

If the journey started off rough and then became calmer then you are doing something about your problems.

You may have started off peacefully and then found it rough going. Take a good look at your life and you may be able to prevent the rough patches becoming rougher!

It is fairly easy, once you know how, to analyse everything about your journey. For instance, if you had a high bank to climb then life is not easy at the moment, but if you climb it with vigour you are prepared to take the bull by the horns and do something about it. If it was a nice sandy bay and you were able to step out of the boat with ease, something in your life is going right. Or could it be that you are taking the easy option? Only you will be able to answer these questions.

The person who met you, was it your spiritual guide, a friend or a member of your family? Frequently it is a stranger and you may be coming face to face with your guide for the first time in your life. Friends and family who are dead very often meet you. Sometimes they are people who are still alive. Whoever it was, they are there to help, so be aware of any messages they wish to impart.

Was your tree a beautiful old oak with a wonderful trunk to lie back on? If it was, you are very lucky. This represents the person you share your life with. If the tree was small or merely a sapling then you are not receiving the support you need. If it was a medium size tree, you are getting some moral support. There is a catch to the old oak tree: you have to look carefully to see whether or not there are dead or diseased branches, not so good!

Do not become blasé about this exercise: it changes every time and you cannot manipulate it. Your higher mind will reveal all.

It is fun to practise this exercise with friends and family and find out what kind of mess they are making of their lives!

Whatever you do don't take yourself too seriously – you will bore yourself and others to death!

FEEDBACK

Date ....

COLOUR EXERCISE

Sit or lie down. Breathe deeply three times, and feel the whole of your body relaxing. You will also feel peaceful. If you have problems relaxing, don't worry. Just go straight into the exercise.

Think outwards towards the universe – you have had a lot of practice already – but don't put any effort into it. The less you force yourself, the faster you will travel! Now ask for the coloured ray you need most, and wait. You will suddenly see a colour in your mind's eye, perhaps many colours. But make no mistake, the spirit colour therapists are usually bang on when it comes to the colour or colours you most need. As your colours become clearer and brighter don't do any more work yourself, just revel in the healing that you are receiving. The rays are perpetually vibrating throughout the universe.

In this dimension the beauty is hidden from us most of the time because of the dense atmosphere. I have seen colours on my astral travels so beautiful they appear to be shot with gold and silver threads – an almost incredible enhancement and one impossible to describe with mere words. These rays are power-ful energies that can flow through matter, as of course does all energy.

Colour is a cosmic force and is essentially spiritual. Dis-ease in the energy counterpart cannot continue when it is regularly permeated by the rays, nor indeed can that in the physical body. The more you practise colour healing, the healthier you will be.

If you want to attract the colour you feel you need, then choose your wardrobe accordingly.

RED   The colour for energy. Breaks up arthritic crystal, releases negative energies within the body, helps the circulation and combats blood deficiency diseases. To aid your visualization technique, think of blood!

ORANGE   Wonderful for people suffering from asthma, fear, depression, and lethargy. Easy to visualize – just think of an orange!

YELLOW   Most definitely the colour for use when meditating. Very spiritual, it brings love and peace into your home and life. It is a purifying ray. To help your visualization, think of a daffodil.

GREEN   The colour for the nervous system, and especially good for muscle spasms. It is soothing – after all it is nature's colour! Choose a shade you feel happy with, for that will be the best one for you. To help you at the start, visualize grass.

BLUE   The healing ray. This is the colour that is always seen when healing is taking place. It calms both the positive and negative electro-magnetic links around the body. Excellent for combating epilepsy, depression, fevers and inflammation, it is the   healing ray *par excellence*. It eases all dis-ease.

VIOLET   The colour for the nervous system, fatigue and emotional problems. Think of violets. Use the blue ray to finish off.

AMETHYST   An excellent cure for insomnia. If you can, find an amethyst stone of beautiful, pale bluish-violet and keep it under your pillow.

PINK   A colour you have to experiment with. For some it works but for others it doesn't. It should bring you peace.

An easy and pleasant way of making sure that you always have the right colour somewhere around your dress is to buy a selection of silk or nylon scarves or handkerchiefs. You can also try beaming colours to friends who need help. Remember, the thought is the deed. Colours can constitute your absent healing chart. They are certainly good for healing at a distance.

As John Ruskin wrote: 'The purest and most thoughtful minds are those which love colour the most.' So good luck!

FEEDBACK

Date ....

*We read that we ought to forgive our
enemies; but we do not read that we ought
to forgive our friends.*

COSIMO DE' MEDICI 1389–1464
(In Francis Bacon, *Apophthegms*, 206)

THE AURIC EGG

There are times when we can't avoid living or working with people who are antagonistic towards us, or whom we find difficult to get on with. This exercise is a safe method of protecting yourself from unwanted outside influences. It closes the aura, and prevents it from absorbing influences from other auras.

First of all, imagine a large egg – large enough for you to walk into. There is a door in it: go through the door and, once inside, fill the oval floor with cushions, so that you have a level surface. Sit or lie down, close your eyes, and relax.

Now, visualize the outside of the egg, the shell, growing harder, including the door. Be sure not to put any effort into this; just *know* that, as you think it, it is happening. Watch the shell becoming impenetrable, and when you are satisfied that nothing can get through stop visualizing and relax for about five minutes. Then you can get up and carry on with whatever you have to do without any worry. This is a good exercise to do if you have to travel on crowded tube trains, too.

FEEDBACK

Date ....

The mind has a thousand eyes,
And the heart but one.

F. W. BOURDILLON 1852–1921
'Light'

BLACKBOARD OF THE MIND

You must now be quite used to being told by me to sit down quietly! Don't worry. The discipline will take you into the wonderful, magical world of the imagination where everything is formed by mind energy. As I have said before many times, and will say again: energy is for ever. It can NEVER be destroyed. You are carving out your own future and the harder you work at it the greater your future will be.

So now, sit down, and when you have relaxed, close your eyes. In front of you, you will see a huge blackboard. On a ledge in front of the blackboard there will be a large piece of white chalk. Pick up the chalk and write on the blackboard everything you hate about yourself and your life. If you can't see yourself writing, just know the words are there. Keep writing. Don't give up until you have remembered everything. If you haven't enough room on the blackboard then turn it over. If you fill that side as well, then ask for another and someone will bring you one. Keep at it. When you are heartily sick of writing down all the miserable things you can remember put down the chalk.

At the side of the chair you will find a table, and on the table a damp sponge. Take the sponge and slowly wipe everything off the blackboard or blackboards. Having done that you will start feeling a whole lot better. You will have wiped the slate clean, as they say. If you do this exercise at least twice a week you will be surprised at how positive you will become, determined that never again will you allow anyone to put you down or make you feel inadequate. Remember you can always put people on your blackboard and have the pleasure of wiping them out!

FEEDBACK

Date ....

I sit and look
around the room
and wonder why
it is that I
have surrounded
myself with all
these meaningless
possessions:
cocktail glasses,
coffee tables,
bits of this and that,
all enclosed by four
brick walls,
a roof and anonymity,
when all I long for
is a timber shack
nestling in the foothills of some
warm and pleasant land,
nudity to free my body
from these tiresome clothes and
to feel my bare feet
sinking in the dewy grass;
one day, perhaps,
sometimes dreams come true,
if this one does,
the only other necessary part
is you.

B.S.

CLUTTER

A cluttered mind is the greatest drawback anyone can have. It leaves no room for new ideas. The rubbish that has accumulated over the years is rolling around creating havoc. This exercise clears the rubbish out of your mind and leaves room for shiny, bright ideas so that your life can take on new meaning.

Sit quietly (once again!). Close your eyes and visualize a room full of tin cans, empty cardboard cartons, old bottles, masses of dirty waste paper. Add a few things for yourself until you have no room to sit down. Now take a broom and start sweeping up. In the corner of the room you will find a pile of dustbin bags. Start filling them up and put them outside for the dustman. Don't moan! If you really want a new life you have to get rid of ALL the rubbish and it isn't easy.

When you have got rid of everything – and I mean everything – start sweeping up all the dust. Now go into the kitchen and you will find a bucket of hot water and a mop. Start washing the floor. Don't stop until your room is sparkling clean. Now relax and look around. Where before it was disgusting, you now have something to be proud of.

This is *your* mind. You have room for all the beautiful things now, don't let it get cluttered up again. It's such hard work putting it to rights.

FEEDBACK

Date ....

102

*Vision or Imagination is a Representation of what
Eternally Exists, Really and Unchangeably.*

WILLIAM BLAKE 1757–1827
A Vision of the Last Judgement

HELPFUL THOUGHTS

Imagination is the key to the Universe. Open the door every day with visualization.

This planet is our responsibility – look after it!

Physical strength, alas, is not always reflected in the mind.

An undisciplined mind will always be the servant of a disciplined mind.

Mountains can become molehills if you take away the rubbish.

The mind is the control tower and only your finger should be on the button.

Do not fog issues with a closed mind.

Treat all animals with respect and compassion.

(*Why not jot down your own helpful thoughts and pass them on!*)

FEEDBACK

Date ....

A CHILD'S FIRST STEPS

A child has grazed its knee and is crying. It comes to me for help. I sit it on a chair, get some cotton wool and bathe the wound with warm water with a little antiseptic in it. I then place my hand, clean of course, over the graze but not touching it, and hold it there for a few seconds. Then I take the child's hand and put it over the graze, repeating the words, 'Heal yourself'. It doesn't matter at all if the child is still crying and has no intention of doing any such thing: just keep repeating, 'Heal yourself'. From an early age you are giving the responsibility of this to the child.

If a child has a headache I do the same sort of thing. I sit it on my knee and put my hand to its head. Then I take the child's hand and place it under mine, repeating 'Heal yourself'. These words will eventually become part of the child's experience and will be totally accepted as he or she matures.

When the child is a little older, say about the age of five, you can add another exercise. Ask it to close its eyes and pretend it has a bowl of cotton wool and a basin of warm water on a table in front of it. Ask it to pretend to dip the cotton wool in the water and clean the wound, then to wipe it with an imaginary clean cloth and put on a plaster. All these operations take place in the child's imagination. What is happening to the child's mind while it is carrying them out?

First of all, the mind energy is expanding. The actions have become a game and the child is releasing from the brain its own endorphins, which are natural painkillers. A child's imagination is very easily stimulated. It will find its fun in the visualization which will eventually become easy. As it goes through the process of cleansing and the rest, the pressure of mind energy is taken off the brain and body and opens up the energy vortices and meridian lines, which in turn enable the child to draw in more life force. Thus the healing process begins. Instead of concentrating negativity on the wound the child will have a positive attitude and the feeling that he or she is in control.

Don't worry if your child doesn't respond immediately. Play games with it every now and then when it is well, then when it is ill, or merely grazed or bruised, it will find it that much easier to put the play into practice.

Parents are always saying to their children, 'Let me kiss it and make it better.' It would be just as easy to say, 'You make it better and this is how we will do it.' Join in the fun, for that is what it is. The younger the child, the more independent it will become, and as it grows up, it will not think it right to leave you, the parent, with all the responsibility.

FEEDBACK

_____

Date ....

Mountains undulating
towards the sea,
where thyme, rosemary,
fennel and wild sage grow.

A snake coiled asleep
in the heather, a rabbit
tremulous and shy,
disappears into a burrow.

A flat rock surface
sparkles with droplets
of water, sprayed from
a nearby stream.

Lizards sun themselves,
occasionally feeding, their
tongues too quick for the
human eye to see.

A rolling stone reveals
a silent toad looking
with baleful eyes at
the intruder.

Its sleep disturbed,
it moves slowly from the
light into the rocks
a little further.

These mountains, so
forbidding from afar,
are alive with every
kind of creature.

They harbour them
from birth until they
die, the cycle starts
again, this is nature.

B.S.

A LAZE ON THE BEACH

Sit quietly, close your eyes and breathe deeply three times. Then imagine that you are standing on the top of a cliff looking out to the sea. The day has been warm and balmy. Now the sun is beginning to set and its beautiful gold-orange glow is shimmering on the water.

Now I want you to take a walk along the top of the cliff drinking in all the beauty. Eventually you will come to a flight of wooden steps leading down the cliffside. Walk down these steps, counting them as you go. There are twenty in all. When you get to the bottom you will see, near the sea's edge, a rock with a flat surface. Sit on this rock and look out over the sea. Now, once again, breathe deeply three times and repeat the following words: 'I feel relaxed, happy and healthy. This is how I want to feel for the rest of my life. This is how I *will* feel from now onwards, all the time.'

After a while stand up, open your arms, and shout your good news to the world: 'I feel so well!' Then climb back up the wooden steps, counting as you go, and when you reach the top walk back to the spot from which you imagined yourself setting off. By now the sun will have set but say to yourself: 'When it rises in the morning my whole life will have changed.'

What will this exercise have done for you? First of all, as you looked at the imaginary sunset, your mind energy will have been projected out and away from your body. Secondly, the scene will have relaxed you by bringing into action your appreciation of colour and beauty. The walk itself will also have been relaxing and stimulating and will have opened up a whole new energy field. When you walked down the steps you will have entered your subconscious being, where negative congestive energies were waiting to be released. Self-hypnosis, in fact.

Remember at all times – you, and you alone, are in control; nobody else. When you reached the bottom of the cliff and sat on the rock looking out towards the sea, you were mentally in a position to give yourself auto-suggestion, with thoughts that would stay in the lower levels of your mind energy. In this stage you can suggest anything to yourself and this will stay with you long after you have forgotten it. You are, if you like, dictating onto a tape from which nothing can ever be wiped out unless you wish it to be. Climbing back up the steps will have the effect of drawing the mind energy back into your body where it will settle itself into position, and as you walk back to the point from which you started you should be feeling a new person.

Remember, this is *your* mind space. Don't allow anyone else in. It is safe and there is no way in which it can cause harm. What it will do is to give you an insight into your own capabilities and a place to which you can escape from problems and perhaps solve a few.

FEEDBACK

Date ....

Géronte:	*It seems to me you are locating them wrongly: the heart is on the left and the liver is on the right.*
Sganarelle:	*Yes, in the old days that was so, but we have changed all that, and we now practise medicine by a completely new method.*

MOLIÈRE (JEAN-BAPTISTE POQUELIN) 1622–73
Le Médécin malgré lui

THE MIND MEDICINE ROOM

Remember, you will be using this room for the rest of your life and it will give you health, happiness and independence. No longer will you visit your doctor for minor ailments, and when you do have to ask the medical profession for help you can hasten your own recovery. In the present state of orthodox medicine, with its endless delays and crippling costs, this is no small benefit.

Whatever you do, please don't skip any part of this exercise because you are building it with mind energy and it will become a pharmacy in the energy dimension and cannot be destroyed. The power of this room will be extraordinary, and like any building it is the foundation that is the most important part.

So here is the exercise:

Once again, sit or lie down, close your eyes and *breathe deeply three times.* When you have done this, I want you to imagine a corridor. Walk along the corridor and soon you will find a door. Your name will be on the door and in the lock you will see a key. Open the door, take the key out of the lock, walk into the room, close the door and lock it from the inside.

Now look around you. This is your mind space. You will find the room furnished with shelves and benches and two windows overlooking parkland. There will also be an easy chair.

This is your pharmacy and your task from now on will be to stock it with whatever you need. So ask yourself what you need most at the present time. Do you get migraines? Are you a diabetic? Do you suffer from arthritis and spend much of your time in pain? Whatever it is, you will now take your first step towards curing it.

Let us assume you are suffering from a simple headache. Sit in the easy chair, close your eyes and picture a jar. Now write 'Headache Pills' on a label and stick it on the jar. Now look inside the jar. By your simple act of labelling, headache pills will have appeared in it, enough to last you a lifetime. So help yourself to two or three of them, put them in your mouth, suck or swallow them and place the jar on the bench. Sit quietly and your headache will go.

Impossible? Not so. But what have you actually done?

By projecting your mind towards the problem and knowing, without any doubt, you are going to be cured, you are releasing your own natural painkillers – endorphins, to be precise. Your mind is controlling the action of the body.

By keeping yourself occupied you have also taken a major step towards independence. By constructing this powerful pharmacy you can cure all your ills. It is a truly magical room.

Visit your Mind Medicine Room every day, whether you are ill or not. Add something every time you enter it. Write more labels to put on empty jars. It is much better to be prepared for any eventuality. One day, it may be a matter of great urgency.

There is no end to the list. Cotton wool, slimming pills, backache pills, hormone pills, heroin or other drugs for addicts. Yes! An addict needs a daily shot while trying to kick the habit. This way makes it a lot easier and can give the same stimulation, for whatever you believe is in the jars, so it will be. What you are building up are energy pills, energy syringes. And everything in energy does exist.

As another example, take the case of a diabetic. He or she walks into the Medicine Room, locks it, takes a syringe from its sterile package in the jar or box and enough insulin from its bottle to last a day. The needle will then be injected into the skin, the skin will be gently rubbed and the syringe thrown away. It will disappear, incidentally – all rubbish automatically disappears. The jar or box will then be returned to its place and the bottle also. The sufferer will now sit down quietly and relax.

A feeling of well-being and expectation will be experienced as soon as the insulin is injected. For the act of injecting it stimulates the energy system which, in turn, stimulates the pancreas. And so the cure begins. Many people find a spirit doctor waiting for them so they just sit down, close their eyes, and relax, while healing is taking place.

Visit your pharmacy for at least five minutes every day, whether you are well or ill. Over the months and years you will probably change things in it. Maybe you will change the benches and shelves and if you are a woman you will want prettier bottles and even some dramatic potions! Time spent in the pharmacy when you are well will speed the cure when you are ill. With this exercise you are building energy, which is power. Its results will change your life.

FEEDBACK

Date ....

Annihilating all that's made
To a green thought in a green shade.

ANDREW MARVELL 1621–78
'The Garden'

REMOTE VIEWING

REMOTE VIEWING 1

1. Find somewhere peaceful where you know you will not be disturbed for at least ten minutes.

2. Sit down in a comfortable chair. Close your eyes and breathe deeply three times.

3. Now, mentally walk to your back door or whichever door leads to the garden. (Do not worry if you have no garden – just mentally leave your home and go to the nearest park, or to a neighbour's garden.) Open the door and walk out into the garden. Walk around slowly, looking at the trees and plants, bend down to smell the flowers if it is summer. Walk over to a tree or bush, or even the garden fence. Touch it, feel the texture. Above all, be observant. You may see things you have not seen before, and if this is so you can always check it physically later. Enjoy the experience.

4. Lie down on the lawn – or, if it is damp, put a cover down and then lie down. Keep the images going. Look up. If there is a blue cloudless sky feel yourself being drawn towards it. If there are clouds, feel yourself being carried away with them. Now mentally close your eyes and *feel* the peace.

5. Now get up and walk back to your house. Open the same door, walk through it and close it. Return to the chair and open your eyes.

   If you have done this exercise correctly, you will now be feeling totally peaceful. If you do not, then you were too tense. Don't worry – it will be better next time.

   If you found that you could not see anything at all, perhaps you will not feel too bad if I tell you that very few people can actually 'see' anything. You simply *know* you are there, you *know* you are looking at the trees and plants, and you *know* that you are touching the trees, bushes or fence.

FEEDBACK

Date ....

REMOTE VIEWING 2

This time you will have to ask a friend or relative's permission to enter their home and you will find it a great help if you have a tape recorder ready so that you can speak into it as you go on your journey. You can then check and recheck what you have seen.

1. Once again, find somewhere peaceful, and sit in a comfortable chair. Give yourself plenty of time for this exercise. Relax, and breathe deeply three times.

2. Visualize your mind energy straining at the leash. Now allow it the freedom to reach out and absorb cosmic forces that will strengthen and revitalize. Watch it as it expands forever outward, *ad infinitum*. Now watch as it returns to you glowing and vibrant. Mentally bring it to the shape of a halo. Again, if you cannot see anything mentally, *know* that it is happening.

3. Visualize the route to your appointed destination. Be quite sure that you know in advance what route you are going to take. You cannot change your route when you are halfway there. Are you going to walk or go by car? If you usually occupy the passenger seat, then imagine that you have your usual driver with you or perhaps a spirit driver.

4. Now prepare to leave your home. Do all the things you would normally do if you were going out. Proceed towards the door and open it, walk through, and close it. From now on, you will be a part of your surroundings. Progress along your chosen route.

5. You have completed your journey. Walk up to the front door and ring the bell. The door will be opened. You will now find yourself in the house, walk around taking in everything that you see or *know* is there. Go all over the building; do not miss anything.

6. Now open the back door if there is one, and walk out into the garden. Try to guess the size. It does not matter at all if your guess is wrong.

7. When you have finished, make your way to the front door and leave, closing the door behind you.

8. Make your way home along the same route. Never take a different route home.

9. Open your eyes. Telephone your friend and describe what you have seen. Although you have visited their home before, things are always changing around the house, and there is bound to be something new.

10. Before you 'travel' to them again, arrange with your friend or relative that they leave something on their dining-room table. Perhaps they would like to try remote viewing themselves. This way you could both practise regularly. It is fun.

FEEDBACK

Date ....

Don't bury me
in soggy damp clay,
that in a short time will
rot me away.

Bury me where the sun beats down;
beneath the dry and warming
ground.

Where my body will slowly dry;
and the gentle rain,
for me,
will cry.

B.S.

BACK TO YOUR ROOTS

I want you to imagine lovely fibrous roots going down into the earth. Feel yourself being pulled down into your chair as the roots grow downwards into the very centre of the earth. *Feel* those roots as they cling to the earth's rich soil. Take your time. There is no hurry. As you identify with the deeply burrowing roots, you will experience a wonderful feeling of security, of being a part of this planet, of simple belonging. Now visualize the fibrous roots thickening until they take on the appearance of tubers. When you can 'see' or 'know' that this has happened, you will be earthed.

Now I am going to ask you to put to yourself two questions which will test how you got on.

1. Did you have a problem seeing the roots as they went down, or knowing that they were doing so? If you did, you are too easily swayed by others, too eager to listen and be carried away by their views.

2. If you had no problem simply watching the roots go down, did you nevertheless find it difficult to persevere and watch them strengthen into tubers? If so, you lack perseverance. You soon get bored with the realities of life, which is the opposite vice to letting reality get on top of you. Therefore you will need to strengthen your own roots before soaring away into the sky. You cannot fly until you are earthed; otherwise, when the moment arrives to 'come down to earth', you will do so with a nasty bump. I have met many mediums and healers who were not earthed – all people who should have known better. They wafted away on cloud nine with undisciplined mind energy, no roots and no direction, and as a result their forecasts and diagnoses were unbelievably stupid. Yet most of them had talent and with careful earthing this could have been used. How sad for them and for the rest of us!

FEEDBACK

Date ....

These things shall be! A loftier race
Than e'er the world hath known shall rise,
With flames of freedom in their souls,
And light of knowledge in their eyes.

JOHN ADDINGTON SYMONDS 1840–93
Hymn

LIFT OFF

I want you to summon up a picture of a field and in that field to visualize an air balloon. Don't strain, but focus your attention on the field. How big is it? Are there trees and if so what sort are they? Is there water around – maybe a pond with ducks and moorhens on it? Or perhaps there are just ditches. Are there cows or sheep in the field? And so on. Let your mind's eye travel freely around, observing all these things. This first stage is vital to the whole exercise because as you let your imagination play, so your mind energy is expanding outwards, linking up with cosmic forces which will have the effect of feeding back to it more strength. Remember too that it is your field and nobody else's! You can see in it what you will.

Now bring your attention to bear on the balloon and the basket attached beneath it. Will you need some steps or a stool to enable you to climb into the basket? If so, put them in place. What colour is the balloon? Look at it carefully and colours will appear. But now you may find you are straining a bit too hard and feeling tension in your shoulders. If so, relax. Breathe deeply three more times. When you have done this, step into the basket. Are there things in it? Note them, if there are. Then settle down comfortably on the seat if there is one. If there is not, then mentally create a chair.

Now imagine the balloon lifting off and savour the sensation of this. Perhaps the ascent will be a little unsteady at the beginning or perhaps it will be quick and straight. Feel the wind on your face, feel the comforting warmth of the sun on your body.

Now look over the side of the basket. There beneath you is the countryside as you have never seen it before. Trees, animals, houses begin to take on an oddly toy-like look. The roads streak like thin ribbons through the villages and fields.

Up and up! Now you are really away and the earth beneath you seems to lose significance as it recedes. There is total peace around you in the clear air and now you start feeling a part of the universe and at one with it. Relax in the warm sun and take in the energy of this wonderful new world which will stimulate and revitalize you.

Healing energies are all around you. Perhaps you will see their beautiful colours as your own mind energy links up with them. In any case your body will absorb them like a sponge. Feel it doing so! And now, ask for help for any problem you may have, whether physical or emotional, and be absolutely confident that someone is listening and that help is at last at hand. Having assured yourself of this (and take plenty of time), think yourself down and return gently to earth.

As you descend, you will feel yourself getting heavier. Once more the roads, houses, trees and fields become distinct. Ease yourself slowly down into the field from which your journey began and, once down, look around it. Has it changed? Maybe a car has been parked in it since you began your ascent and is now waiting to take you home – for remember this is still the realm of the creative imagination.

That is the exercise. It can be practised again and again. Indeed it will have to be practised again and again, for the first time you try it you will almost certainly find that it is rather less easy than it sounds. Here are some questions and comments to enable you to gauge your progress.

1. Did you start on the initial preparations, longing for peace of mind, then decide that the whole thing was more trouble than it was worth and give up? If so, your mind energy was negative, funnelled in and pressing down on the brain as already described, causing dysfunction of the electro-magnetic circuit around your body and producing depression and fatigue. Don't worry! Next time, be a bit tougher with yourself. Force yourself to carry on. You have a lifetime to change in, so what's the hurry?

2. Perhaps you completed the preparations stage but once in the basket, warm and comfortable and with closed eyes, found yourself unable to 'see' anything. Again, don't worry, this is quite normal at the beginner's stage. Just feel total confidence in the progress you have made so far and little by little pictures will start to appear. This is because you are stimulating the mind energy which, as it expands, links up with outside forces which feed back to it increased power and give your mind a helping hand. Moreover if you cannot see when you first start doing this exercise, you can almost certainly feel. One thing leads to another!

3. But if you *can* see, let me help you interpret the messages. The field you saw, was it almost bare of trees and hedges? In that case, you wish to lead as uncluttered a life as possible with the minimum of hangers-on. That sounds a bit selfish and perhaps that is what you are, but who isn't sometimes? As you repeat the exercise you may find yourself adding a tree or two and so be able, back in the everyday world, to tolerate a few more people in your

143

life and even be able to help them. This, however, will be a gradual change. The lasting changes in our lives almost always come slowly and overnight conversions are suspect. If by contrast your field is over-cluttered, then you cannot see the wood for the trees and your life is over-complicated and overcrowded and needs simplifying. If, as you continue to repeat the exercise, the trees in your field thin out, you can be confident that this is indeed the direction in which you are moving.

I hope by now you are beginning to see what this exercise is meant to be doing for you. Its purpose is mind expansion, the improvement of your own life and the monitoring of your own progress by the linking of your own mind energies to the Universal Mind.

4. What were the colours and patterns of your balloon? Check the colour chart in the previous chapter for your own diagnosis. Remember, whatever you need you will attract. If your balloon is a mixture of colours, then congratulate yourself. You are a beautiful balance of the physical and the spiritual. But again, you can monitor your progress every time you do the exercise.

5. What did you find in the basket when you climbed into it? Was it cluttered or uncluttered? Whichever it was, you are now in a position to interpret its state for yourself.

6. When it came to the ascent, did you find take-off difficult? If so, you are afraid of change. You want to feel safe but all you are really doing is imprisoning yourself both physically and spiritually, because where there is fear there can be no freedom, whether of thought, word or deed. Don't worry, 90 per cent of us are cowards at heart. Join the club, as they say. What is important is that you should persevere in your efforts to change. And,

you *can* change, I promise you. But perhaps you went to the opposite extreme and your balloon shot up with alarming speed. In that case, in your everyday life, you are trying to go too fast too soon and failing to attend to detail. Again, with practice, as you continue to repeat this exercise, you will get your balloon to ascend at a more sensible rate and in consequence will find, for the first time in your life perhaps, that back in the everyday world you are noticing all sorts of apparently unimportant things and becoming aware of the emotions of other people.

7. Were you brave enough to look over the side of the basket or did you sit tight? If the latter, you are evidently uninterested in anything except your personal concerns. You are probably also afraid. If, however, you found yourself looking over the side, then you are keenly interested in everything around you, in all the life of the world. Congratulations again! You will not find it difficult to grasp what I have been talking about and to set about your problems accordingly.

8. When you were finally aloft, up there away from the humdrum world and at one with the universe, how did you feel? Did you feel peaceful, or nervous and even afraid? Your answer will show whether the healing powers of the exercise were working on you or not.

9. Did you find it difficult to ask for help? Perhaps you cannot believe that there is anyone out there listening. Let me assure you that given the opportunity your mind energy could be in touch with the Universal Mind permanently.

10. Did you return to earth with a thud, or gently? If the former,

then you were not in control of your mind energy. If the latter, then you are beginning to work along with it.

11. When you returned to earth, did you find that your field had changed in appearance at all – more trees, fewer trees, whatever? If so, then you had begun to make progress in modifying your attitudes even during your first trip. This is great news – provided the progress was in the right direction, of course!

12. When you landed, did you visualize a car waiting in or by the side of the field to take you home? The answer to this one tells you a lot about yourself. The presence of a car suggests that you still have childish attitudes – you want a sweetie for being good. If, however, you are not bothered about transport, that is a sign of independence.

But of course this last comment must not be misunderstood. All mature, well-balanced people have many elements in their make-up. All of us have both a male and a female side and if either is repressed too violently the whole character is thrown out of true. Similarly 'the child is father to the man' and must remain in him to the end of his days. Especially as the child is the source of our imagination. Children have open minds and incredible imaginations, until this is suppressed in the interests of 'reality'. As 'reality' moves in, psychic ability is driven out. That is why so many children become difficult to manage. They, like adults, need their dreams. For after all, what *is* reality? It is worthless except when shaped by imagination just as matter is worthless except when shaped by mind.

So what I am saying is, activate your imagination. That was the guiding idea behind the exercise which you have just read. Each change you make in the pictures you see when repeating it, will modify your actions, your attitudes and the rest of your day-to-day life as you return to it when the experience is over.

Now do you see what imagination is all about? This exercise is also teaching you to discipline your mind so that you will eventually have total control over your spiritual and psychic health and happiness.

FEEDBACK

Date ....

Do all the good you can
By all the means you can
In all the ways you can
In all the places you can
At all the times you can
To all the people you can
As long as ever you can.

JOHN WESLEY 1703–91
Letters: Rule of Conduct

TIME ON YOUR HANDS

So many people are unemployed at the moment, including the young, that I'd like to give them this special message.

Time is something which, when we are busy, we never have enough of. Yet when we do have it, it is so easy to waste! Rather than spending it feeling depressed, people with time to spare could help themselves to a happier future by studying and learning as much as possible. Evening classes are cheap, or if this isn't your style you can borrow language tapes and books from the library – languages always come in useful. You don't have to be good at English; many people who have studied a second language have been able to conquer the grammar better than they did their own!

Using your spare time could, in the long term, enable you to take up a better career when the chance comes along. With more knowledge, you'll have more choices.

Time is precious. Please don't waste it!

FEEDBACK

Date ....

FLY A KITE

If you feel that you are unable to control your emotions then try this exercise.

1. Use your breathing technique, see p. 21. After five minutes you will find yourself standing in the middle of a field high up on the downs. There is a fresh wind blowing against your face and body, and you are having to strain a little to prevent yourself from being moved. Feel this energy that surrounds you and revel in it. There is nothing so stimulating as fighting against the elements.

2. If you look down you will find that you have a kite in your hands. Look at the kite and make yourself aware of its shape, colour and texture because it represents your emotions. Attached to the kite is the cord that will control its flight: this represents your control over your emotions.

3. Lift the kite up and gradually let out the cord, allowing the wind to lift it. As the kite moves up and away from you, keep an eye on it and don't let it out of your sight.

4. It is at this moment that you will feel a release of your tensions as your emotions take flight and release your body from all pressures. You may even find that your eyes will well up with tears as you relax. Set yourself free by allowing the kite to fly higher and higher, but remember, do not let go of the cord! If it strays too high and too far, gently coax it back to a position where you can see it and have control over it.

5. When you feel totally relaxed gradually pull in the cord. The cord is the discipline that you must have over your emotions at all times.

If you do feel emotionally overwhelmed at times, think of the kite flying high and imagine yourself being part of it. With this exercise you must always keep your feet on the ground, but there is nothing to stop your mind waves expanding and linking up with Universal energies.

As you become stronger you will see that the kite looks brighter every time you reel it in. The colours will change with your mood, but they will never revert to the dark colours that you may have seen. You would not allow it!

The shape and texture will also change. You may find the kite is larger than before: that shows that you are becoming stronger, more able to control your emotions. If the kite is smaller, you will have to wait for a little longer for results. The texture may be smooth and silky, showing off your sensual side – don't allow it to become so fragile that it tears! If the fabric is too thick then it won't fly. In time you will find that it will be in between, not too thick and not too flimsy.

Don't forget to record your results each time you try this exercise.

FEEDBACK

Date ....

THE SPIDER'S WEB

Our whole existence begins from one single thread of pure consciousness. Our progression through life depends upon the pattern we weave. It can be a tangled web or it can be spun into a perfectly formed circle. The choice is yours!

This exercise will give you some indication of what your life is like at the moment. It is never too late to untangle your web, or, indeed, if that task is too formidable, destroy it and start again.

1. Begin by clearing your mind of unwanted thoughts. If you find this difficult, imagine yourself under a warm shower. As the water falls about you it is washing the thoughts away.

2. Now imagine a single thread of silk forming in your mind: like the spider you will have an endless supply, so start using it.

3. Begin by attaching the thread to something secure. This will be the centre. Now you are ready to weave. If the thread looks as though it is going to tangle, gently smooth it out. Tangling is not allowed! If you are not proficient enough at imaginative weaving just watch it happen!

4. As your mind clears it will allow the beauty of the web to impinge on your senses. Maybe you will see dewdrops appear, glistening in the morning sunshine. This exercise will show you how much beauty and light you are blocking when your web is tangled. Watch the pattern grow.

5. Do not be misled by the web's fragility – it has a strength that can sustain and support your mind, body and spirit.

6. You may be surprised at the pattern that emerges. It could be simple or complicated. This will give you some idea as to the state of your mind.

7. When your web is complete, record every detail. As you look back over the months, or years, it will help you to assess how much you have improved. This exercise is a must for those of you who find discipline and order a problem!

Each time you practise this exercise the outcome will be different. That is why assessing your progress is so easy.
   Why not finish the poem below when you feel that you have progressed a little? Good luck!

> *This morning I saw a spider's web*
> *Hung with morning dew,*
> *Looking like jewels*
> *Where the sun shone through.*

FEEDBACK

Date ....

The hawthorn hedge puts forth its buds,
And my heart puts forth its pain.

RUPERT BROOKE 1887–1915
'Song'

PEEL AWAY THE PAIN

This exercise will ease pain, stress and anxiety, and at the same time cleanse the whole of the physical body.

Start by choosing a peaceful corner so that you will be able to relax.

1. Gently shake your feet and legs, hands and arms in turn, and finish by gently turning your head from side to side. You should now feel relaxed.

2. Breathe deeply three times.

3. Become aware of the skin that covers your body: think of it as a silken sheath.

4. Now feel this sheath being covered with warm melted wax. As it sets it will absorb pain, stress and anxiety.

5. Peel off this waxy second skin, starting at the top of the head and pulling it down over your feet.

6. Mentally destroy it with all the problems it has absorbed.

7. Your silken sheath of skin should now feel warm, tingly and pliant, and hopefully free of adverse feelings.

   Use this exercise as many times as needed for your particular problem. It really works!

FEEDBACK

_____

Date ....

THE CATHERINE WHEEL

This exercise will generate extra energy and life-force within the physical body. It will harmonize the spiritual side of your nature and enhance your intuitive qualities.

1. Close your eyes and imagine a giant Catherine wheel.

2. At your side you will see a candle and matches. Light the candle and take it over to the Catherine wheel. In the centre of the wheel you will see a fuse – light it and stand back!

3. As the fuse burns, the Catherine wheel will begin to turn. In its centre you will notice that the colour green is prominent – watch that colour.

4. The wheel now starts to gather speed and as it does so it becomes multi-coloured. Red, Blue, Purple, Yellow, Pink, Violet, all the bright colours appear, and last but by no means least, White, Silver and Gold.

5. As you watch the colours they will begin to impinge on your senses and you will find yourself soaking them up like a huge sponge.

6. You may find that tears roll down your face as the energy fills your being.

7. Sparks of light flash out as the wheel continues to spin. Your body will pulsate with light, colour and energy. A feeling of love and compassion will fill your mind and body.

8. Gradually the Catherine wheel loses speed. As it does so the colours begin to fade. At this point your body also begins to slow down and you will feel calm and relaxed.

9. The wheel stops. Silence, Stillness and Peace.

10. Take a deep breath and then open your eyes. You have been recharged and are now able to face another day!

My heart leaps up when I behold
A rainbow in the sky

WILLIAM WORDSWORTH 1770–1850

FEEDBACK

Date ....

*No man can, for any
considerable time, wear
one face to himself, and
another to the multitude,
without finally getting
bewildered as to which is the
true one.*

NATHANIEL HAWTHORNE 1804–64

FOOTPRINTS IN THE SAND

This exercise will help you to retrace your past and bring memories from the subconscious mind to the conscious mind. If you do not like some of the memories then dismiss them, they are of no use to you whatsoever.

1. Close your eyes and visualize a beautiful secluded beach. Blue sky, sun, the sound of the waves. Wonderful!

2. Think of a time in your childhood, one that presents a clear picture. Now take your first footsteps in the sand and as you do so recall that time when you were a child. If there are any unhappy memories visualize the sand absorbing them – you will be free of them for ever. The happier memories you will keep and the sand will retain the footprints.

3. Go through your life year by year – obviously you will have to do this a little at a time – and watch the sand absorbing and swallowing up all the bad memories until you reach the present day.

When you have reached this point you can now start with a clean slate.

Some of the bad memories may have been of your own making – well, at least you're human: join the club! Whatever you may have suffered has to go. You can no longer afford to live in the past – there is such a great future out there for all of us!

FEEDBACK

Date ....

Afoot and light-hearted I take to the open road,
Healthy, free, the world before me,
The long brown path before me leading wherever I choose.

WALT WHITMAN 1819–92
'Song of the Open Road'

ONE STEP AT A TIME

This particular exercise has been tested on those suffering from agoraphobia.

1. Close your eyes and breathe deeply three times. Allow all thoughts to fade into the background.

2. Visualize a place that you have wanted to visit for a long time and have been unable to. Hold a picture of that place in your mind for as long as possible.

3. Whilst you were journeying with your mind you would have found that fear, anxiety and distress were absent. Only confidence, joy and fulfilment were present.

4. Take another mind journey and 'see' yourself opening your front door and taking your first step outside. Look up at the sky, breathe in the fresh air. Look around and take in the scenery that presents itself to you without the prison of walls. As you do this the fear of being outside will diminish.

5. Open your eyes and look around you. Everywhere you will find yourself imprisoned with four walls – very boring!

6. Close your eyes again, visualize the first place you thought of and mentally take your first step outside the front door towards that special place. As you make your journey notice all the things you used to enjoy en route – maybe on your mind journey you will see things you had actually forgotten. Remember your mind is actually travelling. Then you reach your destination, open your eyes.

7. Now prepare yourself for the journey back. Breathe deeply and close your eyes. Think of your home and make your way towards it. You will find the return journey much easier.

8. Open your eyes and look around you. Your four walls will feel like a haven, not a prison, because you now know that you can travel wherever you wish with your mind.

   As you practise this exercise every day you will want to take your first physical steps outside your home. Remember that it is your mind that is in control at all times.

THE THOUGHT IS THE DEED.

FEEDBACK

Date ....

And the rose like a nymph to the bath addressed,
Which unveiled the depth of her glowing breast,
Till, fold after fold, to the fainting air
The soul of her beauty and love lay bare.

PERCY BYSSHE SHELLEY 1792–1822
'The Sensitive Plant'

THE ROSEBUD

This exercise will aid your concentration.

Sit in a comfortable chair and close your eyes.

Imagine you are holding a rosebud in your hands. As you focus your attention on it the bud will begin to open. If you cannot actually 'see' the rosebud, do not worry, just know it is there.

As the petals unfold feel the texture and study the colour; you may find the colour changes as you progress.

Allow the rose to open fully and then absorb the perfume.

At this point breathe in slowly and deeply several times.

Now study the rose again. There may be a few dewdrops sprinkled over the petals. A ladybird may have alighted on it. Use your imagination.

When you are ready, watch the rose close and become a bud again. Then open your eyes.

Only you will have complete control of the rosebud. You will find that this exercise will change every time you do it.

FEEDBACK

Date ....

We are accustomed to see
men scorn what they do not
understand and snarl at the good
and beautiful because it lies beyond
their sympathies.

JOHANN WOLFGANG VON GOETHE 1749–1832

THE MAGICIAN'S CASTLE

This exercise will reveal your innermost thoughts and depth of feeling. Emotions will be unleashed, enabling you to be your own clairvoyant. Close friends will be able to help you to analyse your decisions. You will also find that it is magical.

Give yourself plenty of time for this exercise: you will need to remember each phase as you pass through it.

1. Sit in a comfortable chair and breathe deeply three times.

2. Imagine that you are standing in a field outside the walls of a castle. Take in every detail of the view, the walls, castle, its shape, colour, size, the colour of the sky. Is it night or day?

3. Now walk through the field. Is it full of wild flowers, is the grass long or short, or has it been ploughed?

4. When you have reached the walls of the castle you will find a door in the wall. Is the door open or shut? Notice everything about it.

5. You have to go through the door. What do you see? Is there a path or just another field, or is there a garden? Make your way to the castle.

6. When you reach the castle you walk up to the door. What sort of door is it?

7. Inside the door you will find a stairway. What sort of stairway is it? Remember everything about it. Straight, narrow, winding, steep, wide, short, take it all in.

8. Finally you reach the top. In front of you, on the wall, you will see a painting. Study it carefully and remember everything about it.

9. Turn right and you will see a door leading into a room. Enter. What sort of room is it? Inside the room will be a chair and table – remember every detail about them. Looking around, you will notice a window. What kind of window is it?

10. On the table you will see a box. Remember every detail. Open the lid of the box and place something in it. When you have done this you should feel a warm glow within you.

11. Walk over to the window and look out. Note the colour of the sky. Are there climbing roses on the wall and flowers in the garden? Absorb everything and remember!

It is now time to retrace your steps.

1. Walk out of the room. As you pass the picture study it.

2. Walk down the stairs and as you do so remember every detail.

3. When you walk into the grounds of the castle, look around. What do you see?

4. Walk through the garden to the gate in the wall. Study the gate.

5. Walk through it and when you are standing in the field, look back. What do you see?

6. Walk on and turn back again. You will see a stairway to the Universe. Observe it and remember every detail.

Obviously, I cannot give an analysis for everyone – you will have to do this for yourself. You will also find that your journey differs in some way every time you take it, depending on the circumstances of your life. What I can give you are some clues.

1. The field where you start your journey represents your present frame of mind. For instance, if the field is full of wild flowers, you are feeling optimistic. If it is ploughed then life is a problem. It may be full of thistles, if so you are certainly feeling prickly. If it is long grass, there are still problems within. If the grass is short and easy to walk on, you are coping with your life.

2. The wall represents your day-to-day living. If you can see over it life is, at least, tolerable. If it is too high then your problems, at the moment, may seem insurmountable. Don't worry, if you are really courageous you may want to climb the wall and look over!

3. The gate in the wall represents your partner. If it was large and

heavy going then your relationship is heavy weather too! If it was small and easy to open, maybe you need someone with more character and not a person you can walk all over. If the gate was off its hinges then you have real problems!

4. What did you see inside the walls? Was there a path? Was it another field, or a garden with no path? The path represents your emotional and financial affairs. If it was brick but winding you have problems. If it was an earth path but straight then things are not too bad. If it was rocky, draw your own conclusions. Whatever your path looks like, remember, in time, it can change.

5. The door of the castle. Was it a heavy oak door, or a light door? If it was a heavy door, that would be expected in an old castle. But if the door was so heavy that you could hardly open it, then life is a drag at the moment. If the door was light and easy to open, maybe you are too flippant about your life. The ideal door would be old, heavy, but with wonderful oiled hinges so that it could swing open easily. It represents your attitude to life. Remember, you can always oil the hinges yourself!

6. Were your stairs steep, made of concrete, were they so narrow that you had difficulty climbing them? Maybe they were straight and steep? If you were lucky they were wide and easy to climb. The stairs represent your home life. You can work it out for yourself.

7. The picture. I will leave you to analyse this for yourself. It represents the real you!

8. The room. This represents your hopes and dreams. If your chair was small you are aiming too low. If the table was small – the same. If the view from the window was a garden of flowers then dream on – dreams do come true! If the view was boring, lighten up your dreams and aim higher. The box is the most important thing in the room, however. Whatever you put into the box is the very thing that you have to get rid of – it is spoiling your life! If, as many people do, you put your wedding ring into the box then you must do something about your marriage. The previous answers may give you a clue to what is wrong.

    When you finally retrace your steps you will probably find that everything has altered. This will give you some idea of the benefit you have gained from this exercise.

    Analyse, analyse, analyse, that is the key to your life.

9. The stairway represents your ambitions. The time will come when it will be golden and this will mean that materialism will not be as important as your spirituality.

    The Magician's Castle is truly a magical place. It can change your life overnight!

    Remember to analyse everything. The sky changes colour all the time. Sometimes it's blue, sometimes cloudy and very often dark with stars. This represents how much love and care you need!

FEEDBACK

Date ....

*We are sure to judge
wrong if we do not
feel right.*

ANON

CANCER

I have known people who have cured themselves of terminal cancer with visualization and I believe this therapy should be available at centres throughout the country. Hope is life. Without it we kill ourselves.

Fortunately, there is something more powerful than cancer, and that is the mind. With your mind you can reverse the workings of your body and reduce any tumour to the condition of a trembling jelly. You can knock it for six with your aggression. Are you feeling angry that your body has turned on you? Then let it feel the full vent of your anger in return. Attack the tumour, or the white blood cells, with aggression. Don't give in, fight every inch of the way, and if you have to neglect your home, your family or your friends in order to do so, then so be it.

To deal with a tumour, malignant or benign, the following visualization exercise can be helpful. First, allow yourself about ten minutes of complete peace to prepare yourself for the fight ahead. Now sit down, make yourself comfortable, close your eyes and breathe deeply three times. When you have done this, imagine yourself in a garden. You are standing there in the middle of the lawn, you are wearing very loose clothes and sandals. The sun is coming up and you can feel the warmth penetrating the whole of your body, relaxing every muscle.

Now I want you to walk to the bottom of the lawn where you will find ten steps going down to a terrace. Descend the steps slowly and count them as you go: 1, 2, 3, 4, 5, 6, 7, 8, 9, 10. You reach the terrace and look out towards a landscape of mountains, forests and rivers. This is your mind space. It belongs only to you. It is safe and secure. Remember this. Now, once more, breathe deeply three times.

Then turn right and walk down the terrace, until you find six steps leading down to a smaller terrace. Count the steps as you go. To the right of the terrace is a pool. Remove your clothes and walk into it, sink down into the warm relaxing water, which is also a powerful energy source. As you relax, you will feel your body absorbing the energy and you will begin to feel rejuvenated but still peaceful. Enjoy the pool until you feel ready to leave it, then climb out of it, dry yourself off on the towel by the side of the pool and dress yourself again. Walk back up the six steps, counting as you go. Walk along the terrace and up the ten higher steps, counting again, and return to the spot on the lawn from which your journey began.

Now you are rejuvenated. Your energy fields have opened up. It is the moment to launch your attack. Make yourself comfortable, close your eyes, and visualize your tumour or tumours. You will find a quantity of small pellets in your hand. Insert them into the tumours and when you have done so watch the tumours explode and vanish. Do this exercise as many times a day as you like. Your mind is the most powerful ally you have. MENTAL ENERGY WORKS. Perhaps you can think up even more aggressive things to do. If so, do them. Your tumour won't know what's hit it. Don't give up. Ever.

If you have leukaemia practise a variant of this technique. Travel through the garden and bathe in the pool as before.

Then, instead of pellets, equip yourself with a small vacuum cleaner and travel with it through your bloodstream, sucking up all the cancerous and malignant cells and utterly destroying them. Alternatively, think up an imaginary substance which you can inject into yourself to destroy the excess white cells. Vary the weapons according to your own ideas but on no account despair if you cannot actually 'see' what you are doing. Just to know is enough. With practice all sorts of images will start to appear. Anything can happen, once you apply the power of your mind.

When you have finished your exercise, breathe deeply and imagine a blue healing liquid being poured into the top of your head. As it flows through your body it will take all the debris with it. You will then feel peaceful.

Repeat these exercises every day as many times as you wish. You are at war and there is no way you are going to retreat. Your body is going to do what you want it to do.

Becoming independent and controlling your own health is a wonderful feeling. No longer will you have that awful sense of dependency and being let down by those you trusted.

Above all, make up your mind that you will win. Don't have any doubts. I know you can do it because others have fought and won. Why not you?

FEEDBACK

Date ....

I think I could turn and live with animals, they are so placid and
        self-contained,
I stand and look at them long and long.
They do not sweat and whine about their condition,
They do not lie awake in the dark and weep for their sins,
They do not make me sick discussing their duty to God,
Not one is dissatisfied, not one is demented with the mania of
        owning things,
Not one kneels to another, nor to his kind that lived thousands of
        years ago,
Not one is respectable or unhappy over the whole earth.

WALT WHITMAN 1819–92
'Song of Myself'

PETS: THE WALKING GAME

————————————

1. This is specifically for pets who go out for walks, and in this exercise you will be speaking to your pets whilst they are awake. The first step is taken when you are about to take them for a walk. Look them straight in the eyes and say telepathically, 'Would you like to go for a walk?' Watch the reaction. If they start to wag their tails or rush to the door, then you know that you have reached them. If there is no reaction, try again, but not for more than five minutes. If you get no response at all, then take the animal or animals out for a walk and try another time. Remember, both you and your pets are new to this exciting game, so take it in easy stages.

2. When you return from the walk, look at your pet or pets, and ask them to go and lie down. You may find they will do this anyway, but if you have a particularly active dog, like my own, they will jump up and down to the last, hoping to entice you outdoors again. With this type of animal, telepathy can be very successful. As you know your pets so well, you will also know when you are successful.

FEEDBACK

Date ....

He asks no angel's wing, no seraph's fire;
But thinks, admitted to that equal sky,
His faithful dog shall bear him company.

ALEXANDER POPE 1688–1744
An Essay on Man

PETS: TELEPATHIC COMMUNICATION

---

1. Wait for a time when your pet is asleep. It is much easier to reach the subconscious whilst it is in this state.

2. Close your eyes. Now speak to your pet telepathically. Use the same technique as though you were speaking normally – the only difference is that you will hear the words in your head. Have a loving conversation and assure your pet of your love and respect. Tell it that you will do everything in your power to give it a happy and contented life. Just keep talking. No effort is required; thoughts travel much faster without an impetus behind them.

3. Ask for its cooperation in assisting you by ridding itself of bad habits. Give your reasons as you would if you were speaking to a human.

4. When you have tried this exercise every day for a week, go on to the next exercise.

With this exercise, you can use telepathic communication with as many animals as you wish. They will all pick up the vibrations.

FEEDBACK

Date ....

Time does not stand still,
that which we have left
undone will be so for ever;
that which we leave unsaid
will become thoughts instead
of words; the paths we have
left untrodden will become
tangled with weeds and will
be for ever lost in the
contours of the land; we can
crush the fragile structure
of our lives with doubt,
and those of us who fear
the unknown will be afraid
of life for ever.

B.S.

PETS: COMMUNICATION THROUGH VISUALIZATION

---

1. This is for cats and any other kind of pet. When they are active, talk to them telepathically. If you would like them to stop wrecking your home, then ask them in the nicest possible way. Because cats are so independent, you will have to be very patient and it may take time, but with perseverance you can have good results. You can simply pass on your loving thoughts to the animal and they will feel the vibrations and be more content.

2. When your cat has been out for some time, use telepathy to ask it to return. Let it know that you are going to feed it. Food is always a sure way of enticing animals back home.

3. Visualize the food that you are going to give, then visualize the cat eating it. If your pet does not return the first time, keep trying. The rewards are well worth the effort involved.

Why not use your imagination and visualize your own scenes and reactions? Once you have found the right formula for this talent, try others. You will find it extremely worthwhile.

FEEDBACK

——————————

Date ....

POETRY

To be able to create one must be faced with a blank page!

Poetry should surprise by a fine excess, and not by singularity – it should strike the reader as a wording of his own highest thoughts, and appear almost a remembrance. Its touches of beauty should never be halfway, thereby making the reader breathless, instead of content. The rise, the progress, the setting of imagery should, like the sun, come natural to him.

JOHN KEATS 1795–1821
To John Taylor, 27 February 1818

Poetry comes from the soul. Why not put your deepest thoughts into words? Allow your emotions to spill onto the paper. This will also give you an insight into your own depth of feeling.

O for ten years, that I may overwhelm
Myself in poesy; so I may do the deed
That my own soul has to itself decreed.

JOHN KEATS

POETRY

To be able to create one must be faced with a blank page!

POETRY

To be able to create one must be faced with a blank page!

POETRY

To be able to create one must be faced with a blank page!

POETRY

To be able to create one must be faced with a blank page!

MAKE A LIST OF ALL THE POSITIVE AND NEGATIVE THINGS IN YOUR LIFE

POSITIVE	NEGATIVE

If you have reached this point – great!

If you have reached this point you obviously still have a lot of work to do. Ugh!

MAKE A LIST OF ALL THE POSITIVE AND NEGATIVE THINGS IN YOUR LIFE

POSITIVE	NEGATIVE

If you have reached this point – great!

If you have reached this point you obviously still have a lot of work to do. Ugh!

MAKE A LIST OF ALL THE POSITIVE AND NEGATIVE THINGS IN YOUR LIFE

POSITIVE	NEGATIVE

If you have reached this point – great!

If you have reached this point you obviously still have a lot of work to do. Ugh!

MAKE A LIST OF ALL THE POSITIVE AND NEGATIVE THINGS IN YOUR LIFE

POSITIVE	NEGATIVE

If you have reached this point – great!

If you have reached this point you obviously still have a lot of work to do. Ugh!

In the spaces provided write a brief summary of your day, especially pinpointing irritations. If the same irritations repeatedly appear on your chart week by week then you will have to find some way around the problem to enable you to have a happier lifestyle. In any event you will at least find out what is really bugging you!

SUN

MON

TUES

WED

THURS

FRI

SAT

In the spaces provided write a brief summary of your day, especially pinpointing irritations. If the same irritations repeatedly appear on your chart week by week then you will have to find some way around the problem to enable you to have a happier lifestyle. In any event you will at least find out what is really bugging you!

SUN

MON

TUES

WED

THURS

FRI

SAT

In the spaces provided write a brief summary of your day, especially pinpointing irritations. If the same irritations repeatedly appear on your chart week by week then you will have to find some way around the problem to enable you to have a happier lifestyle. In any event you will at least find out what is really bugging you!

SUN

MON

TUES

WED

THURS

FRI

SAT

In the spaces provided write a brief summary of your day, especially pinpointing irritations. If the same irritations repeatedly appear on your chart week by week then you will have to find some way around the problem to enable you to have a happier lifestyle. In any event you will at least find out what is really bugging you!

SUN

_____

MON

_____

TUES

_____

WED

_____

THURS

_____

FRI

_____

SAT

MANTRIC SOUND

Mahatma Gandhi once said, 'The mantram becomes one's staff of life, it carries one through every ordeal of life. Each repetition of a mantra has new meaning, carrying you nearer to God.'

Mantra comes from the root *man* 'the mind' and *tra* 'to cross', thus mantra enables you 'to cross' the sea of your mind. Our minds are in constant motion, like grasshoppers jumping from one thought to another. By repeating different mantras over and over, we centre our minds on the word and sound, eventually revealing the inner peace that resides in us all. Our fears, conflicts, cravings and resentments are unlocked with this form of song. We can then develop patience, compassion, loyalty and love.

From babies we are taught to feed ourselves, walk, talk and a host of other physical functions. As we grow older and have to train our minds a mass of irrelevant worries and distractions crowd in on us. It is at this point that the practising of Mantra becomes invaluable, concentrating the mind, as it does, on a word or words.

Start by repeating the words in your mind. When you feel peaceful try speaking them out loud. You will find that when you

229

become familiar with the words your mind will conjure them up when you are most in need.

After a while you will want to sing them. This will bring you the greatest benefit of all, as the vibration of sound has powerful healing qualities.

Mantras are especially beneficial for those of you who may suffer from insomnia.

Why not sing them in the bath whilst relaxing, an excellent combination of water and sound!

Those mantras that have been recorded will be marked with an asterisk.*

Don't forget to record your reactions to the mantras on your Feedback pages.

If you wish to learn more about mantras there is a chapter in *Mind Magic* which I am sure will answer most of your questions.

There is nothing to stop you making up your own mantras. Repetition of meaningful words is the key to the power within.

*The root of sanctity is
Sanity. A man must be
healthy before he can be
holy. We bathe first and
then perfume last.*

SWETCHINE

Sum – gar – chardvam
Sum – Vardad – Vam
Sum – Vomanamsi – Janatam
Devarbhagum – Yatha – purve
Sum Janana – upar sate
Samani Vaya Kuti
Samanum Hyridyani Vaja
Samanum Astu Vomano
Yatha Vaha Susahasati

Translation:
Let us move together
Let us sing together
Let us come to know our minds together
Let us share like sages of the past
That all people together may enjoy the Universe
Unite our intention, let our hearts be inseparable
Our mind is as one mind
As we truly know one another and become one.

This mantra was used many times in my daughter Janet's Yoga classes and its beauty never failed to bring tears to one's eyes. It is one of her favourite mantras and I know you will grow to love it too!

* Gold Series Tape 4

FEEDBACK

Date ....

*The first virtue is to
restrain the tongue. He
approaches nearest to the
Gods who knows how to be silent
even though he is in the right.*

CATO

Hare Rama Hare Rama
Rama Rama Hare Hare
Hare Krishna Hare Krishna
Krishna Krishna Hare Hare

One of the best-loved mantras, very well known in the West, this is associated with the Sixties and flower power! It is a powerful mantra with a great depth of meaning.

Hare	–	He who steals our hearts
Rama	–	He who fills us with abiding Joy
Krishna	–	He who draws us to Him

FEEDBACK

Date ....

What is a weed?
A plant whose virtues
have not been discovered.

RALPH WALDO EMERSON 1803–82

OM MANI PADME HUM

This is a great Buddhist Mantram. It means 'Jewel in the Lotus of the Heart'. When repeated many times it allows you to discover your heart centre, opening up the love and compassion therein. This will enable you to pass on the excess to others.

* Blue Series Tape 4

FEEDBACK

Date ....

*Talkative people listen to
no-one, for they are ever
speaking. And the first evil
surrounding those who do not know
the meaning of silence is that
they hear nothing.*

PLUTARCH

CHAKRA MANTRA

Lam, Vam, Ram, Yam, Hum, Aum, Om

This mantra is designed to awaken our energy centres – 'chakras'. It is usually repeated on one note, but can also be spoken. You will find it most effective if you relate each sound to the relevant chakras.

Lam – base of spine (Muladhara chakra)
Vam – below navel (Svadhisthana chakra)
Ram – Stomach (Manipura chakra)
Yam – Heart centre (Anahata chakra)
Hum – Throat centre (Vishuddha chakra)
Aum – Forehead (Ajna chakra)
Om   – Top of head (Sasharara chakra)

   Use one a day to boost your energy level. Repeat four or five times.

* Gold series Tape 4

FEEDBACK

_____

Date ....

There is a pleasure in the pathless woods,
There is a rapture on the lonely shore,
There is society, where none intrudes,
By the deep sea, and music in its roar:
I love not man the less, but nature more,
From these our interviews, in which I steal
From all I may be, or have been before,
To mingle with the universe, and feel
What I can ne'er express, yet cannot all conceal.

LORD BYRON 1788–1824
Childe Harold's Pilgrimage

Jaiya Guru Deva Jai
Jaiya Guru De
Jaiya Guru Deva Jai
Jaiya Guru De

Asharana sharana charana moilay

Translation: Love thy Guru (teacher)

This mantra is especially beautiful if practised in a group.

*   Gold Series Tape 4

FEEDBACK

Date ....

*Truth is the agreement
of the Mind with
Itself.*

PLOTINUS

Asatoma Satagomaya
Tamaso ma Jotygomaya
Vrityo ma Vritillmgomaya

Repeat phonetically.

This mantra can be used when you are fearful. It is protective and calms the mind.

Translation: *Lead me from the unreal to the real*
                Lead me from darkness to light
                Lead me from mortality to immortality

FEEDBACK

Date ....

So many gods, so many creeds,
So many paths that wind and wind,
While just the art of being kind
Is all the sad world needs.

ELLA WHEELER WILCOX 1855–1919
'The World's Need'

Jai Ram Sri Ram
Jai Jai Ramo
Jai Ram Sri Ram
Jai Jai Ramo

Translation: *Love Ram – The Holy Rama*

* Blue Series Tape 4

FEEDBACK

Date ....

Why do you look without
for that which is within
you?

ECKHART

260

A Ram A Ram A Ram A Ram
A Ram A Ram A Ram A Ram
A Jai Ram

Translation: *Love God within you*

* Gold Series Tape 4

FEEDBACK

Date ....

MY LAW – TIEME RANAPIRI

The sun may be clouded, yet ever the sun
Will sweep on its course till the Cycle is run.
And when into chaos the system is hurled
Again shall the Builder reshape a new world.

Your path may be clouded, uncertain your goal:
Move on – for your orbit is fixed to your soul.
And though it may lead into darkness of night
The torch of the Builder shall give it new light.

You were. You will be! Know this while you are:
Your spirit has travelled both long and afar.
It came from the Source, to the Source it returns –
The Spark which was lighted eternally burns.

It slept in a jewel. It leapt in a wave.
It roamed in the forest. It rose from the grave.
It took on strange garbs for long aeons of years
And now in the soul of yourself It appears.

From body to body your spirit speeds on
It seeks a new form when the old one has gone

And the form that it finds is the fabric you wrought
On the loom of the Mind from the fibre of Thought.
As dew is drawn upwards, in rain to descend
Your thoughts drift away and in Destiny blend.
You cannot escape them, for petty or great,
Or evil or noble, they fashion your Fate.

Somewhere on some planet, sometime and somehow
Your life will reflect your thoughts of your Now.
My Law is unerring, no blood can atone –
The structure you built you will live in – alone.
From cycle to cycle, through time and through space
Your lives with your longings will ever keep pace
And all that you ask for, and all you desire
Must come at your bidding, as flame out of fire.

Once list' to that Voice and all tumult is done –
Your life is the Life of the Infinite One.
In the hurrying race you are conscious of pause
With love for the purpose, and love for the Cause.

You are your own Devil, you are your own God
You fashioned the paths your footsteps have trod.
And no-one can save you from Error or Sin
Until you have hark'd to the Spirit within.

ATTRIBUTED TO A MAORI

265

The reward of a thing
well done, is to have
done it!

RALPH WALDO EMERSON 1803–82

CONCLUSION

Know that all these exercises are linking you up with the tidal waves of energy that move the living sea of the universe. Through doing them you are becoming a part of this whole. Feel it. Feel the subtle changes in your body as it leaves the pull of the earth and releases itself from the bonds that tie us to its troubles and cares. You will return, but on your own terms and with the knowledge that you can leave again at will.

Never again will you be a prisoner of gravity. You will become a free spirit. You will have freedom of thought, word and deed, an instinctive knowledge of right and wrong. You will want to simplify your life so that you will have more time to spend on the things that really matter: love, family and friends, and perhaps also to teach others what you have learned so that they may share your spiritual knowledge. You will also find yourself carried away on a wave of audible silence – an experience you will never forget!

If you would like to contact me for help or healing, please write, keeping your letter as brief as possible, to the address below.

Tapes are available: please write for a leaflet to the same address.

Betty Shine
PO Box 1009
Hassocks
West Sussex
BN6 8XS

S.A.E. essential!